BEAUTY OUT OF ASHES

(The True Story of How God Healed Our Marriage and How Gregg Miraculously Cheated Death)

By

Gregg N. Huestis
Emily P. Huestis

BEAUTY OUT OF ASHES—
(The True Story of How God Healed Our Marriage and How Gregg Miraculously Cheated Death)

Published by: Blessed To Be A Blessing Ministries
E-mail: info@b2bablessing.org
Website: www.b2bablessing.org
Facebook:
https://www.facebook.com/blessed2bablessingministries
Ministry Blog: www.b2bablessing.org/blog/
Twitter: https://twitter.com/GreggHuestis67

Published in the U.S.A. by
Blessed To Be A Blessing Ministries
Ft. Collins, CO 80524
All Rights Reserved

Printed In the United States of America

Table of Contents

Dedication

We dedicate this book to **all** *who have helped Emily & I get to the place where we are today. Without all of your help we would have most likely been in divorce court a long time ago...*

There are so many who have helped us during this time of transformation that you are far too numerous to mention...We will make this list short...

First & Foremost: *the Father, Son & Holy Spirit Without Your protection Gregg would not be here to partner with Emily to write this book.*

Our parents: *Roy & Fay Hansen, Tim & Jackie Lawrence, and Joe & Anne Huestis.*

Gregg's closest confidant of over 20 years: *Alex Maddalena.*

Our best friends: *Jason & Suzanne Glaze and Kevin & Christina Richards, Kim Duncan*

The Municipal Court System of Weld County Colorado
(Especially the **Honorable** *Judge John Briggs)*

Intervention & Safe Solutions Treatment Opportunity Program
Mike P.O.
Eran D.V. Counselor.

Gregg's Attorney, *Andrew Bertrand.*

The entire ICU & Med Surg staff of North Colorado Medical Center
in Greeley, CO who worked tirelessly to save Gregg's life.

The thousands of people in the US and around the world who spent so much of their time praying for Gregg's recovery and for our marriage to be restored.

Finally, *to all those who are about to read this miraculous story of God's Mercy, Favor, and Restoration...May the Lord cause this book to be a blessing to you and may He show you the way to receiving the same restoration that we have received.*

--Gregg & Emily Huestis

Acknowledgements

This book **is not** about us...it's about the Wonderful and Miraculous Power of Almighty God and how He took the life of an ordinary couple and turned it around for His glory...To the Father, Son, and Holy Spirit...for without You none of this would ever have been possible.

To Emily P. Huestis -- thank you for your editorial talents, your contribution to the writing of this book, and most of all...your prayers and never giving up on me & our marriage! I love you with ALL my heart and would be wandering aimlessly without you in my life.

To Gregg N. Huestis - thank you for following your heart's desire to write this book & letting me be a part of it...thank you for believing in me & my potential.
I thank God every day for bringing you into my life. I love you!

Introduction

Isaiah 61: 2-4 (TAB) To proclaim the acceptable year of the Lord [the year of His favor] and the day of vengeance of our God, to comfort all who mourn, To grant [consolation and joy] to those who mourn in Zion—to give them an ornament (a garland or diadem) of **beauty instead of ashes**, the oil of joy instead of mourning, the garment [expressive] of praise instead of a heavy, burdened, *and* failing spirit—that they may be called oaks of righteousness [lofty, strong, and magnificent, distinguished for uprightness, justice, and right standing with God], the planting of the Lord, that He may be glorified. And they shall rebuild the ancient ruins; they shall raise up the former desolations and renew the ruined cities, the devastations of many generations.

This is the true story of a married couple who have been on a long journey from ashes to beauty, back to ashes, and *finally* back to beauty once again. It is the real life account of the miraculous restorative power of God at work in an ordinary couple's life. God's restoring power is **so awesome**...He has never left us or forsaken us even in our worst times--Times of personal rebellion. Times of ignorance. Times we allow the devil to totally disrupt our lives. But, despite all this He has never left us or forsaken us.

In the minds of some people, the Christian life is either a bed of roses or a bed of thorns..In reality, however, it is actually both. We often have very blessed times, but we also have our times of tragedy and difficulty. Being a Christian in this world today is not an easy thing. We all face difficulties on a daily basis. We all have tragedies to overcome. The most wonderful part is that He always stands by our side *waiting patiently* for us to repent and run back to Him--To His favor, to His mercy, and to His protection (see Psalm 91). The most important thing to always remember is that the Lord will never leave us or forsake us.

Are we advocating living in sin and rebellion? No, not at all! He is patient and merciful. He will **never** force Himself upon us *or make us obey* His Word. He wants us to be obedient and follow His Word out of heart-felt love for Him and not just because of the consequences or even because of all the blessings that He's promised in His Word. The motivation of our hearts is the most important element to God. He does not want us to serve Him like a bunch of robots. That is why He gave man his own free will to choose to serve God or reject Him.

The choice is up to us how we live. We are the ones who must decide whether or not we will follow God's Word. It is important to note that God does not send *anyone* to hell...**we** are the ones who choose whether we go to heaven or hell. No one can **ever** blame God for sending them to hell. The Lord Jesus has paved the way to heaven. It is our choice and our responsibility to see and accept His way. We must willingly surrender our lives to be obedient to God in His Word. He will *never force us* to follow His direction.

Prologue

John, in the book of Revelation, expressed a powerful truth to us in our generation when he wrote by the Spirit of Grace:

> **Revelation 12:10-11** (NKJV) Then I heard a loud voice saying in heaven, "Now salvation, and strength, and the kingdom of our God, and the power of His Christ have come, for the accuser of our brethren, who accused them before our God day and night, has been cast down. And they overcame him *by the blood of the Lamb and by the word of their testimony*, and they did not love their lives to the death."

Too often, we Christians are embarrassed by our pasts and withhold powerful testimonies of God's grace *that could be used of the Lord to minister to others*, **and deliver them from Satan's grip** (note Romans 6:21 in comparison with Acts 19:18-20 and 1 Corinthians 15:9-10).

I, too, felt this same way *for years*, but I have come to the place where I believe the Lord wants my story to be shared for the benefit of others, that they likewise may find peace through genuine repentance and faith in Jesus Christ.

The Bible clearly tells us: If we confess our sins, He is faithful and just and will forgive us our sins and cleanse us of *all* unrighteousness (1 Jn. 1:9). I realize that my past is a very private, personal situation, and that I am not obligated to tell anyone **anything** about it.

However, I also believe that God has called us to live a life of honor and integrity. This is the reason that I am writing this prologue. I want to thank a friend, Rich Vermillion, for encouraging me to write this testimony, without him even realizing what he was doing.

Freedom from Sins of the Past

For many, one of the most embarrassing things to mention within Christianity is divorce. This is partly because of the strong denunciation of this painful occurrence by well-meaning ministers who seek to deter others from going through this, and partly because of the stigma that is associated with divorce because of such teaching. Though ministers usually mean well when they condemn divorce, they too often cause emotional damage and spiritual "shipwreck" in the lives of those whose hearts have already been wounded. So those people *often hide their past*, even if God's grace brought them out of the messes they once found themselves in.

Consider These Verses of Scripture

Matthew 10:32 (TAB) Therefore, everyone who acknowledges Me before men *and* confesses Me [out of a state of oneness with Me], **I will also acknowledge him** before My Father Who is in heaven *and* confess [that I am abiding in] him.

Romans 10:10 (TAB) For **with the heart** a person believes (adheres to, trusts in, and relies on Christ) and so is justified (declared righteous, acceptable to God), and with the mouth he confesses (declares openly and speaks out freely his faith) *and* confirms [his] salvation.

John 3: 15-21 (TAB) In order that everyone who believes in Him [**who cleaves to Him, trusts Him, and relies on Him**] may *not perish, but* have eternal life *and* [actually] live forever! For God so greatly loved *and* dearly prized the world that He [even] gave up His only begotten (unique) Son, so that whoever believes in (trusts in, clings to, relies on) Him shall not perish (come to destruction, be lost) but have eternal (everlasting) life. For God did not send the Son into the world in order to judge (to reject, to condemn, to pass sentence on) the world, but that the world might find salvation *and* be made safe *and* sound through Him. He who believes in Him [who clings to, trusts in, relies on Him] is not judged [he who trusts in Him never comes up for judgment; for him there is no rejection, no condemnation--he incurs no damnation]; **but** he who does not believe (cleave to, rely on, trust in Him) **is judged already** [he has already been convicted and has already received his sentence] because he has not believed in *and* trusted in the name of the only begotten Son of God. [He is condemned for refusing to let his trust rest in Christ's name.] The [basis of the] judgment (indictment, the test by which men are judged, the ground for the sentence) lies in this: the Light has come into the world, and **people have loved the darkness rather than *and* more than the Light**, for their works (deeds) were evil. For every wrongdoer hates (loathes, detests) the Light, and will not come out into the Light *but* shrinks from it, lest his works (his deeds, his activities, his conduct) be exposed *and* reproved. But he who practices truth [who does what is right] comes out into the Light; so that his works may be plainly shown to be what they are—wrought with God [divinely prompted, done with God's help, in dependence upon Him].

In the previous verses of Scripture, we are told that we must realize [comprehend, understand] we have all violated God's instructions and are worthy of Eternal Separation from God. In other words, the punishment for unrepentant sin is eternal (**never ending**) torment in hell. However, if we repent or openly admit that we have sinned, then we must *confess that sin and turn away from it*. Thus He will forgive our sin, and we will be adopted as part of God's family. Without **true repentance**, there is no forgiveness of sin.

Therefore we will be saved from Eternal Separation from God (love, forgiveness, joy and peace etc.). Does that mean that we will never make another mistake—**No!** It does, however, mean that if we sin, He will forgive us and restore our relationship with Him. In fact, the difference between a sinner and a saint is simple: One **practices** sin and the other **practices** righteousness:

> **1 John 3:4-10** (TAB) Everyone who commits (practices) sin is guilty of lawlessness; for [that is what] sin is, lawlessness (the breaking, violation of God's law by transgression or neglect—being unrestrained and unregulated by His commands and His will). You know that He appeared in visible form *and* became Man to take away [upon Himself] sins, and in Him there is no sin [essentially and forever]. No one who abides in Him [who lives and remains in communion with and in obedience to Him—deliberately, knowingly, and habitually] commits (practices) sin. No one who [habitually] sins has either seen *or* known Him [recognized, perceived, or understood Him, or has had an experiential acquaintance with Him]. Boys (lads), let no one deceive *and* lead you astray. He who practices righteousness [who is upright, conforming to the divine will in purpose, thought, and action, living a consistently conscientious life] is righteous, even as He is righteous. [But] he who commits sin [who practices evildoing] is of the devil [takes his character from the evil one], for the devil has sinned (violated the divine law) from the beginning. The reason the Son of God was made manifest (visible) was to undo (destroy, loosen, and dissolve) the works the devil [has done]. No one born (begotten) of God [deliberately, knowingly, and habitually] practices sin, for God's nature abides in him [His principle of life, the divine sperm, remains permanently within him]; and he cannot practice sinning because he is born (begotten) of God. By

this it is made clear who take their nature from God *and* are His children and who take their nature from the devil *and* are his children: no one who does not practice righteousness [who does not conform to God's will in purpose, thought, and action] is of God; neither is anyone who does not love his brother (his fellow believer in Christ).

A genuine born-again Christian has the nature of God rooted within them, and they will practice *righteousness* as they learn how to walk in Christ. However, by indicating that they are practicing the previous passage of Scripture shows us that they are not perfect at it, and will make mistakes. Like playing a piano, we who are born of God will occasionally hit a wrong "key" and make a terrible sound. But then we pick up where we left off by repenting, and begin practicing again.

Those who are not genuinely born-again, however, do not have that nature within them. They may put on a "show" of righteousness (for example, while at church or when people are watching) but they cannot help themselves from practicing sin and perfecting it because that is their very nature.

So in sharing this, let me be clear that there was a point in my Christian life when I fell away into sin, but the nature of God within me convicted me and eventually drew me back into practicing righteousness once again. I have walked upon the Narrow Way of Christ ever since, and want to use my story to compel others to pick themselves up out of the "mud" of sin through repentance, and to let the Blood of Jesus cleanse them so that they can begin walking with Christ once again. I know the Lord has led to write this testimony and I hope that those reading this can be inspired to admit their faults, turn away from them and be transformed by the Source of all Peace—Jesus!

It's time for me to acknowledge the truth—*And you will know the Truth, and the Truth will set you free.* John 8:32 (TAB).

I have been saved (born-again) since 1 January 1979, at the age of 11. Hence, most of the foolish things I have done in my life have been done either as a believer or as a Christian who got diverted off the path of salvation. Therefore, I am writing this with much regret, **but not condemnation.** I realize where I have come from, and I pray that those who read my testimony will learn that there is forgiveness, restoration and peace, just as I have experienced. During my dark period, the Lord **never** left me. He was always there convicting me of my mistakes and trying to motivate me to come back to His path.

Gregg's Brief Testimony

When I was in the military, while stationed at Ft. Sam Houston in San Antonia, TX, I was unfortunately not following God's instructions for living. While I was there, I met a woman whom I started to date, and became involved in a sexual relationship with her. Due to my Christian upbringing, **I knew this was not right.** I wanted to do the right thing, so I asked this woman to marry me after only knowing her for 3 months. I had a very close friend in the Lord who found out I was planning to marry this woman, and my friend wrote me a letter pleading with me NOT to marry her because we were not equally yoked [not following God's plan for living together, **see 2 Corinthians 6:14 and 1 Corinthians 7:39**]. **Obviously**, I did not listen to my friend, *nor to the Lord.* When we are not correctly following God's plan for our lives, we are often not able to listen to the Lord's direction, which is found in the Bible. I should have seen my friend's letter as a sign from God and ran as far and as fast as possible away from that situation—**but** I didn't!

Things Continued To Spiral Out of Control

Needless to say, we got married. My wife was also a soldier in the military. She had received orders to go to Germany. One day she told me: *"I'm going to go to Germany, if you want to go too, you can— or you can do whatever you want to, **but I am going.**"* My heart sunk! I had orders to go to Ft. Ord, CA and had dreamed of going there for years. The gravity of my mistake had manifested before my eyes with her statement. I didn't know what to do! I had just married this woman, and I believe that married people should not live in separate places if it is at all possible. **So** I put in my paperwork to have "joint domicile" with her in the US military, which was granted. My wife went to Germany and I stayed behind while the paperwork was being processed. I finally arrived in Germany on 8 April 1990. My wife was in a support battalion and was in the field when I arrived in country.

Our relationship was rocky *from the start*, and it became even worse once I arrived in Germany in 1990. My wife regularly withheld love, affection, emotion, sex, etc., telling me that I was emotional enough for the two of us. She was often cruel and would mock me publicly by making jokes. When I would try to tell her how she was making me feel, she just laughed more. I became increasingly miserable, lonely, and depressed. I tried several times to reach out to her, and prayed often that she would hear my heart because I wanted us to work together as a team. Sadly, everything I tried failed. We were not following the same path, just as my friend tried to tell me. Looking back, I wish I had listened.

Enter the first Gulf War...

It was mid-July 1990, just three months after I had arrived in Germany, when my wife received orders to go to the Persian Gulf (Kuwait and Saudi Arabia). This was the beginning of Desert Shield, which later became Desert Storm. It was a huge blow to both of us. We were not happy about her having to go, so she came up with the idea of trying to get pregnant so that she didn't have to leave. For someone who wanted to get pregnant, she surely didn't push the issue of procreation. She was still cold and distant. Looking back, I am very thankful that she did not become pregnant, although I was very upset at the time about her having to go to a combat zone.

She went off to war and I stayed behind working as a medical specialist at a health clinic. While she was gone, I started hanging out in the wrong places and partying almost every night for 7 months straight. I was drinking like it was going out of style. I had opened a door to the devil, which he kicked open wider, and then rushed in like a flood. I tried to separate myself from this lifestyle but I was hopelessly unsuccessful. If we allow bad behavior to start in our lives, it is often nearly impossible to separate ourselves from it—without help from the Lord! As I said previously, I was becoming increasingly miserable, lonely, and depressed. I felt so unloved. Consequently, while trying to fill the void inside, I started frequenting various bars and dance clubs. In the beginning it was just because I didn't want to go home to our empty house night after night and stare at the walls of an empty house.

While my wife was in the Gulf, I heard from several associates that she was living it up before I arrived in Germany as well as that she had been unfaithful. Though she never admitted it, many of the things that were said seemed to answer the questions of why she was so uncompassionate toward me. I became even more distraught, angry, and lonely. I began to feel betrayed. I was an emotional mess, and getting worse by the day.

Without going into any further detail—*I was unfaithful to my wife*. Although, I know I am forgiven, and it is under the Blood of Jesus (1 Jn. 1:9), this is something that is still with me to this day. I could not believe my own behavior. It was so out of character for me to act this way. I was disgusted with myself, and often wished I was dead, although I **never** attempted suicide. I regret my behavior and wish that I had not been so foolish. I listened to the devil—and I got caught in a vicious trap of destruction.

Eventually, I came clean with her and we tried to work it out. However, it became increasingly clear that this marriage was not going to be reconciled. I knew that in order for it to work, we would both have to make some serious changes and each give one hundred percent to making the marriage work. We even went to a female military counselor/therapist for marriage counseling. Sadly, that female counselor did not try to help us reconcile, but merely took sides against me with my wife. I was the center of ridicule between them. I felt like dirt, and neither of them were helping to bring about any kind of restoration—only further condemnation! Since we were stationed in Germany, we were unable to file for divorce with a US court—the military does not preside over divorces in cases overseas. We had to seek an international body to grant the divorce. This was sought, found, and within two months the divorce was final.

The Next Chapter Opens

Soon after, I met a German national and we began to date. However, I was still so messed up emotionally from all that had taken place. She tried to help me get my emotions under control. This woman was far more stable than I, probably because she had a proper European upbringing. After a while, I gave my heart back to the Lord, and she gave her heart to the Lord, for the first time, with me. We were on a new path, a better path, and finally doing it the right way. We got engaged and were later married. However, I still had a lot to learn about marriage though. It was a very difficult adjustment period for both of us, especially me. I had to re-learn that not every woman was out to embarrass me in public, and withhold love or affection. I felt like an emotionally battered spouse. The Lord restored me to the man that I had previously been: faithful, loving, and compassionate. If it were not for His grace and forgiveness and her understanding, I would still be a lost and broken man. Nevertheless, I was determined to learn from my mistakes. To this day, I never want to forget how I felt when I examined my despicable behavior. Why? I never want to **ever** repeat the same mistakes again! I thank the Lord that I **never** have repeated many of my old mistakes. Although our marriage was far from perfect, it got better after the first year. The Lord was working on me and healing my emotions.

Return To The US

My wife & I felt that the Lord was leading us to start our own home health company in Germany. We believed the best way to do this would be for me to further my medical education by going to nursing school in the United States. I contacted my family in Colorado and in mid-December 1998, I went to Ft. Collins, CO to prepare for nursing school. I stayed in Colorado with my father and step-mother until August 1999. I was told by one school that there was no waiting list to start nursing school, but not long after I arrived in Colorado, I found out differently. I contacted a community college in upstate NY, near my hometown, and found that they had not yet selected their students for the nursing program. So I decided to head back to NY to attend nursing school.

During the time I was in Colorado, my wife visited me. I noticed something was different about her attitude. She off-the-cuff mentioned that she had been hanging out with some of our old friends in Germany and had gone to a few dance clubs, among other things. My heart sunk once again. I knew then that was the reason for her change in attitude. I asked her to stop doing this and she promised that she would. However, I would later find out that she was being less than truthful.

We were planning to settle down in Germany since my wife had a well paying job at the Frankfurt Airport. She returned to Germany and I continued to prepare for nursing school. I spent the vast majority of my time studying, going to church, or spending time with my parents. I was determined to better my life by advancing my medical career path.

When I finished nursing school, I returned to Germany. I was greeted at the airport by my wife, but when I went to give her a kiss, she turned her head to avoid it. I was blown away. Later, during the trip home, she proceeded to tell me that she wanted a divorce. I asked her why she didn't tell me this before I came home to Germany. She *hemmed and hawed, changed the subject,* and never really answered my question!

I was committed to our marriage, and I asked if she would be willing to go to counseling with our Pastor to see if we could

XVIII

restore our marriage. She agreed and we spent nine months meeting with our Pastor one to two times a week. During that time, however, something else was occurring. My wife started working extra hours to build up her cosmetic, facial, and massage side business. She seemed to be avoiding me more and more, even while we were trying to "work things out." At the conclusion of our marital counseling, my Pastor sat me down privately to talk. He said he was concerned that we were not making much progress because he had spoken with my wife privately and she told him that she still wanted to end the marriage. My Pastor told me that he felt that I had no other choice but to grant her desire. He said he didn't agree with divorce, but since she had already made this firm decision, it would be best for all to grant her wish and to move on with my life.

I sat down with my wife, and asked her directly if she still wanted to end our marriage—and she did! She also told me that while I was living in the U.S., she had met someone at work but that "nothing was going on" and that she was attracted to this man.

Obviously, my heart was crushed! I had remained faithful, only to hear that my wife was attracted to another man. Most people who have heard this story believe that my wife was **lying**— that she had **already** been unfaithful based on the drastic changes in her attitude and personality. Though she never admitted to any unfaithfulness, it provided me no comfort under the circumstances that prevailed. Jesus said in John 3:20, NKJV, "For everyone practicing evil hates the light and does not come to the light, lest his deeds should be exposed". Consequently, I was being faithful to my wife, however, she did not **appear** to be doing the same in return.

There was nothing more I could do. We had gone to counseling, yet to no avail. Thus, I moved back to Colorado and filed for divorce. Everything was finalized seven months later.

Our story continues...

XIX

1
The Beginning

When Emily and I first met, we were both in the bar scene. I was in the process of getting divorced for the second time. I had recently moved back to Colorado from Germany in May of 2002. Emily and I met in August 2002, and we started to date in mid October 2002.

I felt as though my whole world was falling apart. Although I was far from being the perfect husband, I had dedicated my entire life to my marriage. During this time I was feeling depressed, and I felt like giving up on love and *even* life. No, I was not suicidal, although, I often wished that I was dead. I was confused about where my life was heading, so I would go out to a local country bar to listen to music and visit with people. But, I would rarely drink more than two beers each time I went out. While at this country bar, I met several people who amazingly became close lifelong friends. Two of our friends during this time continue to be two our closest friends today, Jason and Suzanne Glaze.

A fellow nurse friend introduced Emily and I one night at this bar. However, when this friend found out that I was going to date Emily, she told me I should be careful because Emily was "psycho" and all Emily wanted to do was find somebody to marry. Obviously this piqued my interest in Emily even more because I could *see* she really wanted to settle down with a serious relationship--this was *and still is* beautiful to me.

When Emily and I met, she told me she really wanted to get out of the bar scene. She had recently broken up with her boyfriend and had moved in with some friends who partied just about every night. Since this was Emily's unfortunate situation, I asked her if she wanted to move in with me, and we have been together ever since.

Yes, I knew better than to live with someone before marriage; however, due to the situation Emily was facing, I felt this was the best option for her and I to remain together. *I knew the day we met that we were meant to be together.* I sensed this strongly, deep within my spirit, from the day we first met. To this day, **our song** is *"You Had Me From Hello,"* by Kenny Chesney. She literally had me from "hello". I knew, in my heart, Emily was the woman for me, and I wanted to protect her from this kind of lifestyle. I realize that our relationship was very unconventional when it comes to Christian standards, but I felt in my heart this was the best thing for us then. I will not lie and say that everything was wonderful and rosy because it surely was not. Moreover, we **do not** advocate any couple following our example by living together prior to marriage.

As Emily and I got to know each other better, it became clear that she had a difficult past she was desperately trying to overcome. She had been searching for a true friend & partner for many years which she often times would tell me. She also told me she had to kiss a few frogs before she finally found her prince. I, too, had a reasonably checkered past, seeing as I had already been divorced once and was in the middle of my second one. I'm amazed she actually took a chance with me, but, thank the Lord, I'm **really** glad she took a chance by allowing me to be a part of her life. She obviously saw something in me, as I did in her, that led her to welcome me into her life and her into mine.

There were multiple times where Emily tried to leave me because she couldn't handle having someone treat her as well as I did. She was used to being treated poorly by almost every man she had ever been with. The only male who ever treated her well was her stepfather Tim Lawrence. He was her dad, even though he was not her biological father. He was the man who raised her and taught her to never settle for mediocrity. He always told her to find her prince, and not settle for anything else.

Emily not only had difficulty with previous relationships but she would often sabotage those relationships out of fear of gaining and then losing that relationship. When I met Emily, her self-esteem was *very* low. To the outside world, she seemed very confident and strong but, on the inside, she was very weak and timid. The devil had condemned her so greatly concerning her past *that she felt as though she did not deserve to be happy*. This was an enormous roadblock keeping us from being happy for many years. There were times when she would throw stuff, scream and yell, and even threaten to leave me. Emily did leave our house a few times, but the Lord always led her back to us as a couple. I praise God that He did bring her back those times because I have to be totally honest...I don't know what I would do without her in my life. She truly is my soul-mate and my **best** friend on this earth.

One day Emily came to me and told me she had some things that were really bothering her. These were things she tried to "fix" by using and abusing alcohol or finding a new boyfriend. She had an emptiness (a longing) inside her heart that ate at her over and over again for many years. I told her the only One I knew Who could fix her longing was the Lord Himself. I then explained to her about the prayer of salvation and how to pray it. I told her she could pray this privately but I wanted her to let me know if she said this prayer privately.

Miraculously one day, Emily came to me and asked if I would pray the prayer of salvation with her. I prayed the prayer with her. Emily gave her life to the Lord, while I re-dedicated mine to Him. We began to attend a local Assembly of God church and life was going *pretty* good. We were no longer hanging out in the bar scene and we could finally see a great future for us. It was a confirmation for me that the Lord had put us together, just as I felt in my spirit that He had.

The Proposal

Emily & I began to talk about getting married after only dating a few short months. On day we went out to the local mall, the day after Valentine's Day, and I asked Emily to pick out the ring that she wanted. She immediately saw "the one" that spoke to her and we bought it. This wasn't the most "romantic" way of proposing, but this **is** *exactly* how it happened. Emily & I went to the local Old Chicago® restaurant (*I originally remembered it as Pizza Hut® but my beautiful wife clarified this fact for me*), where I asked her to be my wife. I wanted to get down on one knee but she wouldn't allow it. Fearing an adverse reaction, I didn't want her to get embarrassed and walk out so I quietly slipped the engagement ring on her finger and I asked her to be my wife. It goes without saying that she graciously accept my proposal of marriage, and I am extremely joyful that she did.

The Two *Became* One

On 26 July 2003, my beautiful bride and I married. It was a wonderful day, although I must admit, I was scared to death to marry for the third time. So many questions ran through my mind on that day. Will this end up like the other two? Would our marriage survive 10, 20, 30 years only or would we end up spending the rest of our lives together? It **wasn't** that I did not want to marry Emily. Nevertheless, I was scared because I had been down this road two times before and I didn't want to make this mistake *yet* again.

We thank God for Rich Koop, who was the minister who officiated over our wedding. He made us do premarital counseling as a condition for performing our wedding. It was a very nice time of learning even more about each other, as well as a time for us to deal with certain areas that we had not dealt with previously.

We definitely recommend premarital counseling for all couples who are planning on getting married. It is a tool that will help each couple realize the areas that they need to be working on in their relationship. It will also give them an opportunity to fix things before they say "I do."

We have met couples who have quickly said "I do," but often say "I won't" when it comes to making important changes after they have married. This most often happens **if** the couple has not dealt with the weaknesses in their relationship prior to marrying. One of the biggest keys to a successful marriage is to fix the problems **before** one gets married and the problems become worse. Premarital counseling will often help a couple identify the areas of weakness in their relationship so they can address them before they become the undoing of the marriage.

Emily & I, during this time frame, were living outside Fort Collins in a mobile home that I purchased when I moved from Germany. We continued to attend our local church, Timberline Church, in Fort Collins. Life for us was great! We were following the Lord's guidance, but there was still something missing in our spiritual relationship together. It was something we didn't recognize until long after we were married.

October 2007 The New House

One Sunday morning, before we went to church, I was online looking for houses in our area. I found a house near Greeley, CO, which was well within our price range. This was not long before the housing bubble ruptured and the house was incredibly reasonable for the condition of the US economy in 2007. We called a very close friend of ours and asked her to be our realtor and requested an appointment to see the house in person.

We viewed the house later that week, took multiple pictures, and fell instantly in love with the house. Emily & I prayed about purchasing the house and we both felt led by the Lord to make an offer. We settled on a purchase price, and moved in around the first week of November.

Emily & I continued to attend Timberline Church after moving in, even though it was approximately 30 miles one way to go to church. We absolutely loved this church and had been attending since October 2002. However, we were struggling with the driving distance, especially with the price of gas beginning to rise *significantly*. We wanted to find a local church in our area that was just like Timberline, but only closer to our new home.

Once we moved into our new house I began the search for a church like the one we were both used to, and one that was also close to our home. Unfortunately this search turned out to be futile. No matter how much or how hard I searched, I just seemed to come up empty.

I attended a number of churches in the Greeley area, but never found one that I felt Emily & I would both be comfortable attending. Emily was not wanting to check out new churches with me. She trusted me to find a church that we both could enjoy. Emily was raised Irish Catholic, and was used to that quiet, religious environment. When we first started attending Timberline, she was rather taken back by the free, relaxed atmosphere, although she also really enjoyed the freedom that it allowed. I knew she would not be comfortable in a "holy roller" type of church based on her upbringing. Thus, we struggled to find a church that we both could be comfortable with but also would not be a stagnant, religious environment either. I searched our local area for several years and still could not find a church family that we could call home. We did continue to attend Timberline Church, but our attendance became more and more infrequent. In many ways, this was the beginning of our fall from grace.

2
Fall From Grace

Genesis 3: 1-8 (TAB) Now the serpent was more subtle *and* crafty than any living creature of the field which the Lord God had made. And he [Satan] said to the woman, Can it really be that God has said, You shall not eat from every tree of the garden? And the woman said to the serpent, We may eat the fruit from the trees of the garden, Except the fruit from the tree which is in the middle of the garden. God has said, You shall not eat of it, neither shall you touch it, lest you die. But the serpent said to the woman, You shall not surely die, For God knows that in the day you eat of it your eyes will be opened, and you will be like God, knowing the difference between good and evil *and* blessing and calamity. And when the woman saw that the tree was good (suitable, pleasant) for food and that it was delightful to look at, and a tree to be desired in order to make one wise, she took of its fruit and ate; and she gave some also to her husband, and he ate. Then the eyes of them both were opened, and they knew that they were naked; and they sewed fig leaves together and made themselves apronlike girdles. And they heard the sound of the Lord God walking in the garden in the cool of the day, and Adam and his wife hid themselves from the presence of the Lord God among the trees of the garden.

As we previously stated, Emily & I met in the country bar scene. Our fall from grace *began with* hanging out in the bar scene more and more as time went on. It was not a dramatic departure from the norm for our lifestyle, but rather a very slow *and gradual* processes (See Gen. 3:1-8). The devil rarely tempts one to go hog wild in the exact opposite direction that one was previously on. He gradually pulls us away ever so slowly until we are so far away from center *that we can't remember where or how* this departure actually started.

The enemy **rarely** comes against us with *obvious* changes that are easy to spot as sinful and evil. He tries to lure us away *ever so slowly*, much like how crab are cooked at a seafood restaurant, the water becomes warmer and warmer ever so slowly until the crap is cooked. If one were to think one *cannot be deceived* by the enemy and tricked into gradually turning away from following the Word of God and His direction, then one would be arrogant, and ignorant of the enemy's devices. Emily & I are able to write about this very situation because of personal experience. It can and all too often *does happen* to even the best of believers. We're *not implying* that we were super Christians by any means. Still, we are living proof of how the devil gradually and slowly causes one to steer off course by deceiving us into doing things that *could* and eventually **would** derail our spiritual progress. **The devil cannot make us do anything**! All he can do is tempt us into listening to his lies and following his word *instead of God's Word*. If one stumbles and falls into sin, it is <u>**never**</u> God's fault or the devil's...it is *always* our own fault. The responsibility for our sinning *always* lays upon the decisions that **we** make. This is just a plain fact that every one of us needs to face and accept the consequences for our actions.

Who's To Blame?

James 1:13 (TAB) Let no one say when he is tempted, I am tempted from God; for God **is incapable of being tempted** by [what is] evil and He Himself <u>tempts **no** one</u>.

8

Emily and I were lonely and looking for other friends. We had our best friends, Sue & Jason, 13 miles from our home, but they had their own *lives and we could not expect them to always have time to hang with us.* We also had not found a church close to our home and did not have very many friends to be accountable to for our decisions, Christian or otherwise. We began to go out **drinking** to two local bars in our area a few times a week. This gradually increased to 3 and 4 times some weeks over a lengthy period of time. At our worse condition we *were not* hanging in the bars 3-4 times a week consistently. Nevertheless, we were compromising far too much **and would eventually pay the price for our actions.**

I used to live near Frankfurt, Germany for 12 years. Over there, it is totally normal for born-again Christians and even their pastors to hang out together after Bible study, church, dinner or a prayer meeting and have a beer or two. I'm not saying it was normal to drink until one was 3 sheets to the wind. However, this was a normal lifestyle for me and my Christian friends and I rarely thought twice about it. That is why it was *perfectly normal* for me to go out to a country bar, have a beer or two, and go home later that evening perfectly sober and not think twice about it. I would always stop drinking at least 2 hours before I was leaving to go home so that I would not end up with a DUI on the way home. For all intents and purposes, I was considered by most as one who drank responsibly.

As time went on, we were frequenting these establishments more often and we were ultimately drinking increasingly more. Obviously, it didn't start out this way at first. In the beginning, we were both drinking much like I used to when I moved back to the US from Germany. Moreover, at times, we would by a 6 pack of beer and drink at home 1 or 2 nights a week **long** *before* we started to frequent the local bars again. This unfortunately eventually increased to a 12 pack 1-2 times a week. This was shortly before we returned to the bar scene and ended up paying a *much higher price*.

Nevertheless, we gradually began to increase in our alcohol consumption, which was especially true for Emily. Additionally, there was something very ominous brewing **deep inside** Emily's soul that had not yet become apparent. Sadly, we *both* have an *addictive* personality about us. We have always been **very much** the type of people who live by the motto: *"go big or go home"*. I was not **always** as responsible with my drinking as many thought. Granted, *most* of the time I would only drink a few drinks and then drink water or cola the rest of the night, so that one of us was sober to drive home. Unfortunately, that was not ***always*** the case.

Fall From Grace Accelerates

On the night of 24 April 2012, Emily & I were at one of the local bars to celebrate a friend's birthday. Everything was going reasonably well until I realized it was about 9:30 pm and I needed to go to work the next day. I told Emily that it was late, and we needed to get home because I had to work in the morning. Emily, who was heavily intoxicated, protested my decision to leave. I then proceeded to tell her I was leaving and if she wanted to ride home with me she needed to get into the truck, but Emily declined. So, I went home and started to get ready for bed and for work in the morning. About 60-90 minutes later, Emily had gotten a ride home. She came in the house and the argument picked up where it left off when I left the bar.

We both had had way too much to drink and were not thinking clearly *whatsoever*. Emily was very angry with me for leaving her at the bar, and she began to yell at me with her arms up in a boxing stance. I tried several times to get away from her without a far worse confrontation, but every time I tried to get away she would be right there in my face, mirroring my every move. I became more and more frustrated by her boxing stance and her refusal to allow me to walk away, and without thinking clearly I pushed her away from me so I could get out of the house. When I pushed her, she fell across our large sectional couch and onto the floor in a face plant. She became even more angry with me regarding my behavior. I am not proud of my behavior **in any way**. In the heat of the moment, I was only thinking about getting away from the situation. I obviously was not thinking that if I pushed Emily away from me she could fall and possibly get hurt. Perhaps I didn't realize she was as intoxicated as she was. I'm honestly not sure exactly what I was thinking during this situation. As I said earlier, I was intoxicated and was not thinking clearly. I know this though, if I would not have been intoxicated, I would have never pushed my wife. Moreover, I know that if we both had not been intoxicated this whole incident would never have taken place. Alcohol was the fuel that kept this fire burning and therefore this domestic issue. A few short minutes later, the police showed up at our house. I was arrested and taken to jail charged with Domestic Violence. I spent about 14 hours in jail until I was bailed out by my father the next afternoon once I was arraigned before the Honorable Judge Briggs.

At my arraignment, I was informed of the charges filed against me, of which I didn't like nor agreed with. It was not a pretty sight, to say the least. Moreover, I was informed that I was not allowed to return to my home or have contact *of any kind* with Emily. I had to have my parents go to my house and gather up my belongings. It looked as if we were headed for divorce court. At this time, I wanted to be away from Emily and didn't know if I wanted to even attempt to save our marriage. I also had no idea what was going through Emily's mind. I assumed that she wanted nothing more to do with me and I might as well cut my losses and move on. Our world was falling apart again. We were back in the state of ashes yet again. I had no idea if God would save our marriage, much less if He wanted us to stay together, for that matter. I was once again in a state of confusion with no end in sight.

During my period of incarceration I called my parents in New York and asked them to call my office to tell my boss that I had a family emergency to and would not be in to work until at least the following day. I certainly did not want to have someone else tell my boss that I was in jail, nevertheless why I was sitting in jail. I was embarrassed, to say the least. I wanted to be the one to face the music and break the news to my boss. I also was not sure if I would continue to have a job with this domestic issue in play. I found out later that Emily had called my office to give them a heads up that I was not going to make it into work the next day because I was in jail.

While I was in jail, I ended up getting *schooled* regarding being incarcerated by my cell mate Greg...*just writing those words makes me cringe*. Yes, my cell mate's name was Greg too, what are the odds of that? I was told by Greg and some of the other inmates not to admit to pushing my wife or I would be found guilty *automatically*. Being raised in a Christian home as I was, I wasn't comfortable with **not taking responsibility** for pushing my wife. I also felt I had pushed Emily *in self-defense* because I was honestly scared she was going to kick my behind into next week. I could not possibly see why I would be found guilty of domestic violence. I thought I wasn't going to need a lawyer because I hadn't done anything illegal. I hadn't done anything illegal...had I? *I was wrong*!

Facing The Greatest Challenge of My Life

Once I was released from jail, I received a call from my best friends, Jason & Suzanne. They wanted me to come by their house to talk about the legal implications of my being incarcerated for domestic violence. They advised me that I was extremely foolish if I decided to not secure an attorney to defend me against these charges. I must confess...I was very tempted to go it alone due to the lack of finances and *especially* because I felt I was innocent of all these charges, since I thought had acted in self-defense. I really believed that I was innocent until proven guilty, *at least that is how I understood the legal system from watching TV*.

My friends helped me see that I was being ***ignorant* of the seriousness of these charges** and that if I didn't secure an attorney, I could end up facing a fine of up to $5,000 and possibly 18 months in jail on top of a huge fine. I took my friends' advice and secured the attorney they recommended. Andrew Bertrand, my attorney, agreed to take my case and assured me that he would assist in answering these charges and would be able to help me to have my record sealed and these charges ultimately expunged, since I had no former arrest record and the charges waged against me were misdemeanors.

Nevertheless, I placed this whole thing in the hands of the Lord. I prayed, "*Lord, I cast the whole of my care, regarding this legal issue, upon You, and I entrust the circumstances of it to* **Your** *care. Thank You Lord for directing this situation in the way that* **You** *want it to go. I thank You for a Supernatural miracle involving it and for Your healing power to be in this situation. In Jesus Name, Amen (So be it).*"

3
Live Like You Were Dying

In the previous chapter, Emily & I wrote about how we ended up in the middle of one of the greatest battles of our life together. However, that was until things got even more serious.

The day was 30 April 2012, and I had finally returned to work for my home health company following a few days off to try and get my wits about me once again. I was just about finished working for the day when I made one last attempt to call a man I was trying to admit to our agency. I was able to get in touch with him and he gave me his correct address.

On this day, I happened to be riding for work on my brand new 2011 Yamaha Road Star. It was a very hot day for April and I was not wearing my helmet due to the heat. Prior to leaving my office, I programmed my phone's GPS with this gentleman's address and mounted it to my motorcycle's handle bar. I was riding on Highway 34 heading east toward 47th Ave in Greeley, CO. I was staring at the GPS on my phone when I *suddenly* looked up to see the traffic light and realized it was green but the cars were not moving through the intersection.

I Got A Wake Up Call From Heaven

I do not remember much more about the accident from this point on, but I will tell you what I faintly remember and have been told from others who witnessed it. It appears that when I looked up at the traffic light I realized the cars in front of me were not moving so I attempted to slow down by applying the front and back brakes together. However, for some reason, I only grabbed the front brake, something I was taught never to do by my father who has been riding for over 50 years, and held on for dear life. The bike began to skid approximately 20 feet (based on the skid mark left on the road) as the front brake locked up. I was then thrown a reported 50 feet in the air onto the shoulder of the highway.

EMS was called and I remember briefly being in the back of an ambulance. I recall asking one of the paramedics why I was in the ambulance, and he told me I had been in a serious motorcycle accident. It was later reported to me that I told the paramedic I was fine and I could not go to the hospital with him because I had a client to admit to my agency. I also told him that I would be in a lot of trouble if I didn't complete the admission. The paramedic said I was fixated upon my need to go see this man and admit him to our agency. It seems he was able to convince me to go with him to the hospital, *but only* as long as he promised to have someone call my office to notify them that I had been in an accident and rushed to the hospital. Obviously, I was not in the best state of mind at this point in time.

I was taken to the ER at North Colorado Medical Center for further assessment and treatment of my obvious injuries. Later that afternoon, I was transferred to the Intensive Care Unit (ICU), and my parents were notified that the doctors *did not* expect me to survive the next 48 hours. The doctors sent me to have a CAT Scan which revealed that I had a severe concussion and a subarachnoid bleed, which is a bleed inside the skull that was putting increased pressure on my brain. This increased pressure was causing my vital signs to be unstable. According to my medical records, when I first arrived in the ER, my blood pressures were running between 162/102 - 200/120 with pulse rates in the low 100's. I was in and out of consciousness, confused, extremely agitated, and had little to no memory of any part of this situation.

I had road rash all over my face, abdomen, hands, and

head. I also broke 6 ribs on my left side. According to the ambulance records, I lost about 500 milliliters of blood (which is approximately the size of a 12 oz soda bottle). I was a mess...*literally*! I later found out that I told the ICU nursing staff to "leave me alone, I am a nurse, and I can take care of myself". To say the least, I had a serious head injury called a Traumatic Brain Injury (TBI) and I remember very little of what I said and did.

After approximately 30 hours in ICU, I was transferred to the surgical floor because my condition had stabilized but I still required frequent care. I later had one of the nurses from the ICU come visit me and ask if there was anything they could have done to make my care better. I told her they did an awesome job and to please apologize to the ICU staff for my erratic behavior. I felt terrible for how I had acted even though I knew it was caused by my TBI. I still felt very embarrassed by my unchristian behavior. I stayed on the surgical floor until I was discharged from the hospital 1 week later.

Emily was not able to be with me during the first few days I was in the hospital due to the Restraining Order (RO) that was automatically put into place under Colorado State Law, due to the domestic violence charges pending. The police officer who investigated my accident came to see me at the hospital and asked if I wanted my wife to know about my accident. I said yes! My wife quickly petitioned the court to be allowed to be by my side during this extremely dangerous time and she was granted her request.

Below is a letter that my beautiful wife, Emily, wrote to me the first night I was in the ICU. She wrote this letter to me out of heart-felt love because she was not allowed to see me yet due to the RO. I had **no idea** that she had made the decision to fight for our marriage **the day before my accident.** This is so beautiful and touched me so deeply (it makes me tear up every time I read it) that I wanted to share it with all of you to bless you as I was blessed.

17

My Dearest Gregg,   5/1/2012 **0056**

I am writing this as I am sitting in the garage listening to one of your favorite bands: DAUGHTRY! **You are right now in NCMC ICU fighting for your life!**

The doctors say that the next 4 days are going to be critical! I know that you can fight this! You are too stubborn to give up too easy! I can't be there in person with you because of the restraining order but I hope that you know I am there in spirit! Besides your parents, you have had a lot of friends come visit you and more to come see you. Kevin, David, Sue, and Jason have come to visit you. Katie and Good Bob should come see you later today!

There are so many prayers and thoughts coming your way right now that I think GOD is getting overwhelmed! I am doing my fair share of prayers too!

I LOVE YOU WITH ALL MY HEART! I AM SO SORRY FOR WHAT TOOK PLACE LAST WEEK! I want to ask for your forgiveness and I hope that you will give me another chance! **I am fighting for our marriage!** I don't want to lose you! GOD brought us together 10 years ago for a reason and I am not giving up on that! I believe that we had to hit rock bottom ***to realize that we both have things we need to fix! I hope that you feel the same way!*** Neither one of us gives up too easy! We fight for what we want!

I want you to know that I am making changes within myself to make our marriage better!

I have decided that I need some professional help in dealing with my abandonment issues with my biological father. I have my first counseling appt. on Thursday. I also have an appt. with Dr. Watanabe next week and I am going to talk to him about possibly increasing my medications. *I am going to definitively cut back on my drinking!* I have realized that I have been self-medicating with alcohol and ***I can't do that anymore!***

Hopefully you can see that I am trying to make things better. We were so happy for the first 6-7 years of our marriage. Remember when people used to ask us how long we were married and we would tell them several years. *They were shocked because they figured we were newlyweds because of the way we acted!* **<u>I want that back!</u>** I don't know how we got off that path but ***I would like us to get back on that path!***

I don't know when you are going to be able to read this but I wanted you to know my feelings on everything and where I stand! If you don't want to fix this and want to move on in another direction, I totally understand!

I LOVE YOU WITH ALL MY HEART!

Your loving wife,
E

Once Emily was able to be by my side, we began to talk and started to work out some of our differences. She stayed with me for 4.5 days except to go home and take care of things. **This was the beginning of our restoration.**

During this whole situation; the accident, the restraining order against me and my not being able to be by my wife's side, I got a new appreciation for life. My eyes were opened in many wonderful ways. There is a song that became very real to me during this time. Its message so permeated my being that it almost became my anthem for living.

A Song That Became Real Life To Me

Live Like You Were Dying

He said: "I was in my early forties,
"With a lot of life before me,
"An' a moment came that stopped me on a dime.
"I spent most of the next days,
"Looking at the x-rays,
"An' talking 'bout the options an' talkin' 'bout sweet time."
I asked him when it sank in,
That this might really be the real end?
How's it hit you when you get that kind of news?
Man whatcha do?

An' he said: "I went sky diving, I went rocky mountain climbing,
"I went two point seven seconds on a bull named Fu Man Chu.
"And I loved deeper and I spoke sweeter,
"And I gave forgiveness I'd been denying."
An' he said: "Some day, I hope you get the chance,
"To live like you were dyin'."

He said "I was finally the husband,
"That most the time I wasn't.
"An' I became a friend a friend would like to have.
"And all of a sudden goin' fishin',
"Wasn't such an imposition,
"And I went three times that year I lost my Dad.
"Well, I finally read the Good Book,

"And I took a good long hard look,
"At what I'd do if I could do it all again,
"And then:

"I went sky diving, I went rocky mountain climbing,
"I went two point seven seconds on a bull named Fu Man Chu.
"And I loved deeper and I spoke sweeter,
"And I gave forgiveness I'd been denying."
An' he said: "Some day, I hope you get the chance,
"To live like you were dyin'."

Like tomorrow was a gift,
And you got eternity,
To think about what you'd do with it.
An' what did you do with it?
An' what can I do with it?
An' what would I do with it?

"Sky diving, I went rocky mountain climbing,
"I went two point seven seconds on a bull named Fu Man Chu.
"And then I loved deeper and I spoke sweeter,
"And I watched Blue Eagle as it was flyin'."
An' he said: "Some day, I hope you get the chance,
"To live like you were dyin'."

"To live like you were dyin'."
"To live like you were dyin'."
"To live like you were dyin'."
"To live like you were dyin'."

This is a very powerful song written by one of country music's biggest stars, Tim McGraw. The song spoke to my heart **very** deeply. I have always loved this song but it *became alive* to me when I first heard it after my accident. I finally realized what the meaning of this song was. I realized that it was about focusing on what is *really* **important**. My attitude toward life, and things that happen in it were **instantly** changed. I was no longer as irritated by the small stupid, insignificant things that used to get to me. I suddenly felt free! Free to focus on what was the most important thing in my life after my relationship with the Lord...**my marriage**!

Reading Emily's letter and hearing this song for the first time after my accident made me realize just how close to death I truly was. It was freeing and frightening *all at the same time*. I had cheated death by His hand, and I could not understand why He allowed me to live as He did. I questioned Him about this. I certainly did not want to wreck my motorcycle and spend a week in the hospital. This motorcycle accident was just that...an accident, *not an "on purpose."*

Nevertheless, I was extremely sad and depressed. **I** had possibly caused my marriage to fall apart **all by my stupidity in pushing my wife**. I was angry **at myself**, my behavior, and the fact that I thought I had basically torn my marriage's foundation down **with one stupid move**. Although I was never suicidal, I felt like I didn't want to live. I was the one solely responsible for harming and hurting my wife: physically, emotionally and even spiritually. I was so embarrassed by my behavior...the drinking, fighting and pushing my wife. I knew better than to allow myself to get into something such as this. Yet, the Lord had mercy on me and touched my wife's heart restoring our marriage...**we are truly blessed**

4
Present Day

We are so glad that we have finally arrived at this portion of our true story...**it's the restoration part**. It's where we are currently living today. Despite all of the terrible things that happened from 24 April to 2 May 2012, God *never* gave up on us. He was working on both of us behind the scenes.

In the beginning of my court dates, I was very angry. I felt falsely accused of domestic violence. I thought "*I only pushed Emily. She has literally slapped the snot out of me more than once and nothing has ever happened to her. So why am I the one who had to go to jail, be kicked out of the home he pays for, and be forced to find some other place to live?*" I was really angry at Emily, as well as at my **stupid** self. I just couldn't get past my feelings of being persecuted for "defending myself". That is until I read the State of Colorado statute on Domestic Violence.

Domestic Violence As Defined By the State of Colorado

"The definition of domestic violence varies depending on the context in which the term is used. A clinical or behavioral definition is 'a pattern of assaultive and/or coercive behaviors, including physical, sexual, and psychological attacks, as well as economic coercion, that adults or adolescents use against their intimate partners.' Legal definitions across the States generally describe specific conduct or acts that are subject to civil and criminal actions, and the specific language used may vary depending on whether the definition is found in the civil or criminal sections of the State's code.

Approximately 46 States, the District of Columbia, American Samoa, Guam, the Northern Mariana Islands, Puerto Rico, and the U.S. Virgin Islands define domestic violence in their civil statutes. These statutes typically are found in domestic relations laws but also may be found in family or social services laws, and they provide a means for victims of domestic violence to obtain civil orders of protection and other protective services.

Domestic violence can be defined as 'attempting to cause or causing bodily injury to a family or household member or placing a family or household member by threat of force in fear of imminent physical harm.' Other terms used across the States include 'abuse,' 'domestic abuse,' and "family violence.' While the specific language used by States to define domestic violence varies considerably, 24 States, American Samoa, Guam, and the Northern Mariana Islands define domestic violence as the occurrence of any of the following acts:

• Causing or attempting to cause physical or mental harm to a family or household member

• Placing a family or household member in fear of physical or mental harm

• Causing or attempting to cause a family or household member to engage in involuntary sexual activity by force, threat of force, or duress

•   Engaging in activity toward a family or household member that would cause a reasonable person to feel terrorized, frightened, intimidated, threatened, harassed, or molested

Approximately 40 States, Puerto Rico, and the Virgin Islands list in their statutes specific acts that constitute domestic violence. Most common among these are sexual assault, assault or battery, causing physical harm or serious injury, threatening or placing a victim in fear of harm, harassment, stalking, trespassing, damage to property, kidnapping, and unlawful restraint. Approximately 11 States and Puerto Rico include child abuse in their civil definitions of domestic violence. The civil definitions in Colorado include violence or threatened violence against an animal that is owned by a victim of domestic violence, and injuring or killing an animal as a means of harassing a person is considered domestic violence in Nevada.

Approximately 34 States, American Samoa, Guam, and Puerto Rico define domestic violence in their criminal or penal codes. These definitions generally describe acts that can lead to arrest and misdemeanor or felony prosecution.

In criminal laws, domestic violence may be defined as 'any criminal offense involving violence or physical harm or threat of violence or physical harm' committed by one family or household member against another. Other terms used across the States include 'domestic assault,' 'domestic battery,' 'domestic abuse,' or 'assault against a family or household member.' The specific language and terminology used by States in criminally defining domestic violence varies considerably.

Approximately 16 States, American Samoa, and Puerto Rico list in their statutes specific acts that constitute domestic violence. Most common among these are assault or battery, sexual assault, harassment, stalking, trespassing, kidnapping, and burglary or robbery. Arizona, Utah, and American Samoa include child abuse in their criminal definitions of domestic violence. Animal cruelty is included in the criminal definitions in Arkansas."

Legal Definition of Domestic Violence In Colorado?

"In Colorado, domestic violence, for the purpose of a civil protection order, is defined as:
• Any act of violence or threatened act of violence against you, your children under 18 and any animal owned by either of the parties or by a child of either of the parties;*
• Examples of behavior that may qualify as domestic abuse:
  ○ Name-calling;
  ○ Threatening or harassing phone calls;
  ○ When the abuser threatens to injure himself;
  ○ Threatening to physically or sexually abuse your children;
  ○ Threatening to use a weapon against you;
  ○ Threatening you by threatening to harm animals;
  ○ Threatening you by following you;
  ○ Threatening you by damaging property;
  ○ Throwing things;
  ○ Grabbing or pushing you;
  ○ Forcing sexual contact upon you;
  ○ Physically or sexually abusing the children in your household;

o   Slapping, punching, kicking, biting, choking or otherwise physically harming you; or

o   Forcing you to stay in a closet, room, house, or any other location against your will.

To be considered domestic violence as defined under Colorado law, the person who acted abusively toward you must be someone:

•   Who is or was related to you by blood or marriage;

•   Who lives or has lived with you; or

•   Who you have or had an intimate relationship with.* You do **not** have to have sex during the relationship for it to count as an 'intimate relationship.'***You can read the exact legal definitions on our CO State Statutes page.* Colo. Rev. Stat. § 13-14-101(2) ** See Colorado Protection Order Form JDF 401, Incident Checklist, available at http://www. courts.state.co.us/Forms/Forms_List.cfm/For m_Type_ID/24 *** *People v. Disher*, 224 P.3d 254 (Colo. 2010)".

Once I read the above definitions regarding domestic violence, I realized how guilty I *truly* was. It doesn't matter what Emily did...good OR bad. It only matters what I did. According to the Colorado State Law, **I was guilty of committing domestic violence**. That was a huge, hard pill to swallow, so to speak. I had to face up to my actions. I had to take full responsibility for my behavior. I could not hide behind feeling threatened by her or my rationalization of self-defense.

I posted this post on Facebook® in June 2012. I wanted to share it with you:

Emily & I have been dealing with some things recently that **very well could have destroyed us**

individually and as a couple. I firmly believe that sometimes we either open a door to the enemy (which is most of the time how he gets into a believer's life) and other times the Lord seems to allow us just enough rope to hang ourselves, but He NEVER LEAVES OR FORSAKES US!

I DO NOT believe the Lord *tries us with evil or teams up with the enemy to cause us to be spiritually attacked as some have taught*. WE ARE **all too often** the ones who allow the enemy an opening...**even though often we may have no idea that we have done so**.

This is where one's endurance and commitment to the Lord & His Word are tested. It is in these times where we either fall upon the Stone in humility and repentance *or the Stone falls upon us*.

However, I have to report that we have ONLY grown closer to the Lord and to each other. We are surely not glad for the adversity BUT we are VERY happy for the results. We are VERY thankful to the Lord for His FAVOR & MERCY, that through these adversities Emily & I have become the closest to Him & to each other that we have been in our entire 10 years of being together.

God has used the things we have been dealing with *to work an incredible work inside of us individually and as a couple*. I plan to write a book detailing what we have been going through: **the good, the bad, & the ugly**. BUT, mostly focusing on the good that has grown out of the bad & the ugly. And I plan to focus on the things the Lord taught me personally through my near fatal motorcycle accident. Obviously the Lord spared my life for a reason.

I often questioned him regarding why He protected me from death in the early days after the accident. But, NOW I can **clearly** see why His Hand was upon me to protect me from the enemies' attempt at taking me out of this world.

The doctors told Emily & my parents that they did not expect me to survive the first night. BUT...Praise the Lord...<u>I'm still here</u>, and I am in as good and possibly even better physical, and ESPECIALLY spiritual shape than I have been in a very long time. God has used this situation to cause us to readjust our priorities: mentally, emotionally, and most importantly spiritually.

We are not glad **for the adversity**, but we are VERY grateful **<u>for the results</u>**.

If we had to go through all of this again...KNOWING the results, we would **GLADLY** endure IT ALL again.

We DO NOT believe God CAUSED it to come into our lives (*we allowed some things to slip which caused it to manifest*), but we are THRILLED at the way the Lord has caused all these things to be turned around to bless us...especially when WE DIDN'T deserve it. His Love, Mercy & Favor have endured in our lives for many years.

Looking back at ALL of the many things He has delivered me personally out of...I am so grateful to Him that He has always had such a WONDERFUL and STRONG Presence upon my life. I say this **NOT** because I am special, but rather because **HE is SPECIAL** & **MERCIFUL**!

The Lord bless & keep all of you,

Gregg & Emily Huestis

Here is another post I added to my Facebook® account in June 2012:

The Direction of Blessed To Be A Blessing Ministry

Some may not understand the decision my wife, Emily, and I made to purchase another motorcycle **only 6 weeks after** my near fatal accident. I can understand this.

On the other hand, one must also understand the following: I have been a born-again Christian for almost 34 years. I have been following the Lord's leading intently *for the vast majority of the time.* Have I missed...**oh, without a doubt.** But, the Lord has NEVER lifted His merciful and gracious Hand off of my life.

The Lord started dealing with me in regards to a motorcycle ministry in the late 80's. At that time I had no idea if this is where the Lord was directing me or not. I just knew that my passion for ministry and for motorcycles would one day come together...in what way would that take place is still yet to be seen.

Due to some recent events (which I will not go into at this time) which my wife & I have been dealing with, we have prayerfully decided to put the motorcycle ministry on the back burner for the time being. We are going to spend our time in ministry within our local church, Northern Colorado Cowboy Church, as well as working on my next two books. The Lord called me into the ministry at the age of 14, and I know He has Anointed me to preach the Word of God. I DO NOT say this with arrogance IN ANY WAY! I say this in faith because I KNOW the vision the Lord placed in my spirit at the Morris Cerullo World Evangelism Partners Seminar at Chicago, Il in Sept. 1983. I remember this experience like it was yesterday, that's how strong it still burns in my spirit.

To what extent, that also remains to be seen. I have always felt that I would be used in a ministry traveling the globe teaching & preaching the Word of God and building up the Body of Christ. I have always had a passion to strengthen the Body of Christ because IT has been so messed up in its doctrine and experiences for many years. That being said...keep us & Blessed To Be A Blessing Ministries in your prayers for the Lord's direction and His timing for public ministry, and know that we will also be working in some sort of capacity in a motorcycle ministry in the future...

Lord bless & keep you all,

Gregg & Emily Huestis

The Results

Emily and I are not proud of our behavior, **whatsoever.**

On the other hand, we would both **gladly** go through this whole situation again, **if we knew that at the end of the day we would be experiencing the relationship that we are experiencing now**. This situation, as awful as it was, has brought Emily & I into a far closer relationship with the Lord and with each other than we have ever had together. We are the happiest we have been in our entire lives. God knew exactly what He was doing with this situation. This situation was caused solely by our stupid behavior. We had gotten off His path. But, He had His hand upon us the entire time. He wanted us to get things straight with Him and with each other. He allowed us to mess up our life together so badly that we had no other direction to look **but up**! This was not His fault whatsoever...it was our fault....pure and simple.

Emily & I had started marital counseling prior to my being sentenced for domestic violence. However, once I met with my probation officer, Mike, I was informed that under Colorado Law, a person in domestic violence classes *is not allowed to be in couples counseling at the same time*. I had a **huge** problem with this because Emily & I were doing **so well** in our counseling and I didn't want to mess that up. We were meeting with a born-again counselor, which we recommend to every Christian couple who needs counseling. I was not willing to violate the terms of my probation, so I contacted our counselor and informed her that we needed to suspend our counseling while I was in the domestic violence classes. Emily, as you have read in the previous chapter, is in personal counseling to work on her problems.

Epilogue

I am now in domestic violence classes so that I will learn how to **never allow** anything like this to **ever** happen again. I have learned so many effective tools to properly handle confrontation. One of the assignments that my counselor gave our group was to write a letter of apology to the person that we offended. She told us that we didn't have to share it with that person. However, I felt I owed Emily the opportunity to read this letter, which she did. Emily really appreciated the letter and we decided to include it in this book.

My Letter of Apology

Dear Em,   4 Sept. 2012

I have been thinking a lot about all that **I** have done to get us in this situation. In the beginning, *without a doubt*, I **was** thinking that I had not done anything wrong and that you provoked me into behaving the way that I behaved.

I have since done a great deal of thinking and even looking into the legal meaning of domestic violence. **Wow, was my thinking all messed up!** I have since realized that I am guilty as charged, as the day is long. My eyes have been opened to the reality of what I have done to you, and how much I have hurt you.

This is why I am writing this letter of apology to you. I can now comprehend how stupid and foolish I was for hurting you. I pushed you that awful night, knocking you to the ground. When I did this, I not only hurt you physically, but also emotionally, mentally, and even spiritually. There are so many foolish things I have said and done that I need to ask for your forgiveness.

In the last few months I have fortunately come to realize that there is **ABSOLUTELY no excuse** for my behavior (not only the night I went to jail but the many times I have behaved inappropriately toward you *verbally* in public & private). As far as the night I went to jail, the truth of the matter is that you didn't do anything that provoked me into my behavior. The responsibility for us being in this situation **solely** lies upon my shoulders. There is no justification for my behavior **whatsoever.** I chose to drink and I also chose to act inexcusably toward you that night. I made bad choices and ended up reaping the consequences of my behavior, *as I rightly should have.*

I also realize that I have not always treated you with dignity and respect. At times I have embarrassed you by jumping on you for being intoxicated and saying things I felt were better not said. Therefore, I **have not** been the best husband to you, someone you could be proud of and thrilled to have in your life. My behavior by doing these things was inexcusable and **I take** full responsibility for them. You do not deserve to be disrespected as I have done in the past. I am working daily on this to not allow myself to behave this way, *no matter if I don't agree with your comments.*

As you know, I have been attending domestic violence classes for the last 2 months and I have been learning how to spot the triggers to my anger <u>so that I can get better control over myself</u> **before** I go off the deep end by acting like a fool and either hurt you with my words or my hands. I've been learning to take a "time out," or, in other words, how to step away from the situation so that I can get my thoughts better under control, so that I don't lash out at you in anger. You do not deserve to be treated this way **ever.**

I have also realized that I have often lashed out at you verbally and been controlling about situations. For some reason, I didn't know how to come out and tell you how I was feeling about the situation(s) we were dealing with at the time, instead I acted out in anger toward you. This, of course, is **no excuse** for my behavior **whatsoever.** I should have just been open and totally honest with how I was feeling instead of acting like some ignorant Neanderthal. You are my equal, and **never** my subordinate.

I have also been learning empathy, or how to have compassion and put myself in your shoes, so to speak, and think about how my actions **made you feel**. I've been learning how to see a situation from another's viewpoint and not just be selfish and only look at it from my perspective.

I am *beginning* to understand how I made your feel that night and how I have made you feel other nights when I have allowed my mouth to say hurtful things to you. I say that I am beginning to learn this because I don't claim to have "arrived" or that I am perfect now. I'm a work in progress, **but I am determined to continually work faithfully**

**at becoming a better person, and husband to
you.** I have set some personal goals for myself
since attending these classes.

I have also come to the realization that I need to
quit drinking alcohol **FOR GOOD**. Not just
because of the RO that's in place, **but for the
betterment of our relationship**. It's obvious that I
was intoxicated and out of control the night I hurt
you. That is **in no way** an attempt to justify my
behavior, rather it was a wakeup call for me that if I
want to have you in my life and have a healthy
prosperous marriage, it is imperative that I remain
alcohol free.

I did not realize that I was far more verbally
aggressive with you when I was drinking. As we
discussed a few weeks ago when I apologized to
you for being snippy a few days prior, you told me
that I was tame compared to how I acted several
times before when I had been drinking. Hearing
that made it even more clear to me that **I needed
to quit** drinking alcohol for good because I had not
realized that I was being so mean to you then.

I want to tell you more about my goals for
treatment. These are the things that I am working
on changing and improving. I still have a ways to
go (I realize this), but <u>I am determined to reach
ALL of my goals and to continue to live by these
goals for the rest of my life</u>. I'm not doing any of
this *just* because of the RO (although this is
required of me) or to "win you back". I'm doing
them because they are the right things to do and
they will help me to be a better person and
husband.

This reminds me of a song by Chris Young, "Wanna Be A Good Man." I can SO relate to the song especially when it comes to our relationship...

I wanna be a good man
A "do like I should" man
I wanna be the kind of man the mirror likes to see
I wanna be a strong man
And admit that I was wrong man
God I'm asking you to come change me
into the man I wanna be...

...I wanna be a stay man
I wanna be a great man
I wanna be the kind of man **she sees in her dreams**
God, I wanna be your man
and I wanna be her man
God, I only hope she still believes
In the man I wanna be

Perhaps this song may seem "cheesy" to an extent. However, it is one of my favorite Country songs **and it says what I have not always been able to say**.

My Goals For DV Treatment

1. Accept FULL responsibility (accountability) for my actions and this situation without assigning blame to anyone except myself.
2. To NEVER forget that my actions **do** have consequences that I **must** face and deal with.
3. To learn to listen better to you & not try to always get in the last word or "win" the argument.

4, To learn to communicate better with you and be empathetic (think about how my words will make you feel so that I don't say things in the wrong way and hurt you or be selfish).

5. To learn to take control over my thoughts and insecurities so that they do not dictate my behavior.

6. To learn to let go and allow you to feel more freedom to do things that you like and not just what I believe is the "right" thing to do.

7. To not allow my insecurities to control my actions (to be open and honest about how certain things make me feel).

8. I want every kind of abuse out of my life (there is NEVER an excuse for being abusive. No one deserves to be treated with such disrespect as I have done in the past).

I **now** am understanding, more and more, that I should not have behaved in this situation and many others with anger, **and blaming you for how I was feeling**. I, <u>**and I alone**</u>, am responsible for how I allow myself to feel. No one and no situation has the power to make me do anything. **I, and I alone, am the responsible person for my actions**.

I have spent a considerable amount of time praying and asking the Lord to help me to learn and change, and learn how to better communicate with you and others. To learn to always treat you ONLY with empathy, compassion and love, and to no longer respond to you with anger and violence: verbally as well as physically. I will never put my hands on you again in a violent manner. I have set myself to keep this goal for the rest of my life. I will also not allow alcohol to be a factor in my life again.

I said all of this to ask you this...Would you **please forgive me for hurting you**: physically, emotionally, mentally, and spiritually? You are a smart, wonderful, and beautiful woman. You **do not** deserve to be mistreated by me in any way. I have been such a fool to hurt you! I love you with ALL my heart, Gregg

A Fresh Start

I am **so proud** of my wife for taking the steps that she has taken to improve herself and for not giving up on me or our marriage. I would not have blamed her if she chose to, but I am **so grateful** that she decided not to do this. I owe her an eternal wealth of gratitude for all of this. We are both back in church on a regular basis. We are attending Northern Colorado Cowboy Church, and our pastors are awesome. The Spirit of God in our services is so sweet, and we feel at home in our church.

Moreover, due to the recent events with my probation, we have decided to put the motorcycle ministry *on hold for now.* I was advised by my probation officer to avoid the very appearance of wrong doing while I am on probation. Why? It's because it does not take a **huge mistake to cause one to violate the conditions of one's probation.** The system is just geared this way. and has been for many years. Therefore, since the motorcycle ministry we want to associate with has ties to reaching the 1%ers of motorcycle clubs, we have decided it is best to avoid this at least for the moment.

Emily & I have a new "our" song. It's a very powerful song lyrically by the band Daughtry. The song has a powerful message that really applied to our relationship.

Start of Something Good

you never know when you're gonna meet someone and your whole wide world in a moment comes undone you're just walking around then suddenly everything that you thought that you knew above love is gone

you find out it's all been wrong all my scars, don't seem to matter anymore coz they lead me here to you

i know it's gonna take some time but i've got to admit that the thought has crossed my mind this might end up like it should i'm gonna say what i need to say and hope to god that it don't scare you away don't want to be misunderstood but i'm starting to believe that this could be the start of something good

everyone knows life has its ups and down some day you're on top of world and one day you're the clown

well i've been both enough to know that you don't wanna get in the way when its working out the way that it is right now you see my heart; i wear it on my sleeve coz i just can't hide it any more i know it's gonna take some time[From: http://www.metrolyrics.com/start-of-something-good-lyrics-daughtry.html]but i've got to admit that the thought has crossed my mind this might end up like it should i'm gonna say what i need to say and hope to god that it don't scare you away don't want to be misunderstood but i'm starting to believe that this could be the start

coz i don't know where its goin' there's a part of me that loves not knowin' just don't let it end before we begin you never know when you're gonna meet someone don't wanna be misunderstood but i'm starting to believe that this could be the start coz i don't know where its goin' there's a part of me that loves not knowin' just don't let it end before we begin you never know when you're gonna meet someone and your whole wide world in a moment comes undone

i know it's gonna take some time but i've got to admit that the thought has crossed my mind this might end up like it should i'm gonna say what i need to say and hope to god that it don't scare you away don't want to be misunderstood but i'm starting to believe that this could be the start of something good

We give God **all** the glory and thanks for the restoration of our marriage. He has taken two ordinary people who were heading the wrong direction, and has restored something that was once ashes but now is a relationship of beauty.

The Path To Forgiveness, Restoration, And Lasting Peace

Are you suffering with the pains of your past? Here are some wonderful passages from God's Word to bring you comfort, wisdom, and healing:

Proverbs 2:6-12 (TAB) For the Lord gives skillful *and* godly Wisdom; from His mouth come knowledge and understanding. He hides away sound *and* godly Wisdom *and* stores it for the righteous (those who are upright and in right standing with Him); He is a shield to those who walk uprightly *and* in integrity, That He may guard the paths of justice; yes, He preserves the way of His saints. **Then you will understand righteousness, justice, and fair dealing** [in every area and relation]; yes, you will understand every good path. For skillful *and* godly Wisdom shall enter into your heart, and knowledge shall be pleasant to you. **Discretion shall watch over you, understanding shall keep you**, To deliver you from the way of evil *and* the evil men, from men who speak perverse things *and* are liars...

Proverbs 3:1-8 (TAB) My son, **forget not my law *or* teaching**, but let your heart keep my commandments; For length of days and years of a life [worth living] and tranquility [inward and outward and continuing through old age till death], these shall they add to you. Let not mercy and kindness [shutting out all hatred and selfishness] and truth [shutting out all deliberate hypocrisy or falsehood] forsake you; bind them about your neck, write them upon the tablet of your heart. So shall you find favor, good understanding, *and* high esteem in the sight [or judgment] of God and man. Lean on, trust in, *and* be confident in the Lord with all your heart *and* mind and do not rely on your own insight *or* understanding. In all your ways know, recognize, *and* acknowledge Him, and He will direct *and* make straight *and* plain your paths. Be not wise in your own eyes; reverently fear *and* worship the Lord and turn [entirely] away from evil. It shall be health to your nerves *and* sinews, and marrow *and* moistening to your bones.

Proverbs 16:1-6 (TAB) The plans of the mind *and* orderly thinking belong to man, but from the Lord comes the [wise] answer of the tongue. All the ways of a man are pure in his own eyes, but the Lord weighs the spirits (the thoughts and intents of the heart). **Roll your works upon the Lord [commit and trust them wholly to Him; He will cause your thoughts to become agreeable to His will,**

and] **so shall your plans be established *and* succeed.** The Lord has made everything [to accommodate itself and contribute] to its own end *and* His own purpose—even the wicked [are fitted for their role] for the day of calamity *and* evil. Everyone proud *and* arrogant in heart is disgusting, hateful, *and* exceedingly offensive to the Lord; be assured [I pledge it] they will not go unpunished. By mercy *and* love, truth *and* fidelity [to God and man—not by sacrificial offerings], iniquity is purged out of the heart, and by the reverent, worshipful fear of the Lord men depart from *and* avoid evil.

God's Perfect Will for us is that we live and act according to His Wisdom. His Wisdom is His Word (the Bible). When we make God's Word first place and final authority in our lives, it changes **the way we think and act.** Thus, we begin to think **His thoughts** after Him. And as our testimony reveals: If we try to live without His Wisdom guiding our lives, we will **only** end up living **broken** lives. However, our testimony also reveals another truth: If we will turn to God in true repentance, and put our total trust in Him by living according to His Word, He will exchange our messes for His blessing, and turn our lives around for His Own glory:

Romans 3:23 We have ALL sinned and fallen short of the glory of God (paraphrased).

Romans 6:23 (TAB) For the wages which sin pays is death, but the [bountiful] free gift of God is eternal life through (in union with) Jesus Christ our Lord.

1 John 1:9 If we confess our sins He is faithful and just to forgive us our sins and cleanse us of *all* unrighteousness (paraphrased).

God tells us that acknowledging our sins (*lying, stealing, taking the Lord's Name in vain etc.*) is the first step on the path to forgiveness, restoration, and lasting peace. In order to experience these wonderful gifts, we must repent of our sin (confess it to the Lord and turn completely away from all wrongdoing). Put our trust in Him as the sacrifice for our sins through His Own suffering upon the cross, **and obey Him completely as** our Lord and Savior. **Then ask Him to** change us into a new person.

When we do this, He will come into our lives, spiritually speaking, and will change us. He will cause us to think His thoughts, which are found in His Word [the Bible], and **He** will change us into **a brand new person**. All of our past sins are cancelled at once; in His eyes, it never happened. He washes us clean, and releases us from all guilt of our past. He sets us free from our sins and gives us the power to live in a new way and power to follow His direction—thus our lives will be successful and have new purpose.

A Closing Word of Encouragement

Emily & I hope and pray that this book has been a blessing to you. We also hope that by sharing our testimony it has encouraged you to not give up on your relationship. God miraculously restored our marriage. If He can do it for us, He can do it for you too.

An Important Message

Dear Reader,

We believe it was no accident that you have come across this book. We want you to know that the Lord Jesus loves you and wants to bless your life in every area possible. He wants to give you **peace** and **joy** like you have never experienced before. If you desire to accept His free gift, we invite you to pray the following prayer:

"Dear Heavenly Father, I come to you in the Name of Jesus, and I ask you to forgive me of all of my sins. You said in Romans 10:9&10, that if I confess with my mouth the Lord Jesus and believe in my heart that You raised Jesus from the dead, that I would be saved (born a new).

I believe in my heart that Jesus is the Son of God. I believe He died on the cross for my freedom from sin and evil. I believe that You raised Him from the dead so that I would have a right relationship with You. I accept Jesus as my personal Lord and Savior. Jesus come into my heart and change me into the person You want me to be. I give you my life today.

Father, I thank You for accepting me as a member of Your family. Thank You for giving me Your peace and joy. I thank You for blessing every area of my life. Help me to live for You. I ask all these things in Jesus Name. Amen!"

If you have just prayed this prayer, accepting Jesus as your Lord and Savior, please email us at: **info@b2bablessing.org.** We would love to hear from you and help you grow in your new faith in Christ.

—Gregg & Emily Huestis
Blessed To Be A Blessing Ministries

www.ingramcontent.com/pod-product-compliance
Lightning Source LLC
Chambersburg PA
CBHW021222020426
42331CB00003B/428